SHORT TALES
Fables

The Lion and the Mouse

Adapted by Shannon Eric Denton
Illustrated by Mike Dubisch

WAYLAND

First published in 2014 by Wayland

Copyright © 2014 Wayland

Wayland
338 Euston Road
London NW1 3BH

Wayland Australia
Level 17/207 Kent Street
Sydney, NSW 2000

Adapted Text by Shannon Eric Denton
Illustrations by Mike Dubisch
Colours by Wes Hartman
Edited by Stephanie Hedlund
Interior Layout by Kristen Fitzner Denton and Alyssa Peacock
Book Design and Packaging by Shannon Eric Denton
Cover Design by Alyssa Peacock

Copyright © 2008 by Abdo Consulting Group

A cataloguing record for this title is available at the British Library.
Dewey number: 398.2'452-dc23

Printed in China

ISBN: 978 0 7502 7833 1

Wayland is a division of Hachette Children's Books, an Hachette UK company.
www.hachette.co.uk

One day, a bored mouse was watching a sleeping lion.

The mouse decided it would be fun to surf down the lion.

So the mouse slid down the lion's leg.

Suddenly, the lion woke up
and saw the mouse.

The lion caught the mouse with his paw.

'Please, please let me go!' the mouse begged.

'I'll do anything to pay you back!' the mouse cried.

14

The lion found the mouse's begging funny.

'Okay, you may go' the lion said.

That afternoon, the lion
continued on his way.

He was soon trapped in a hunter's net.

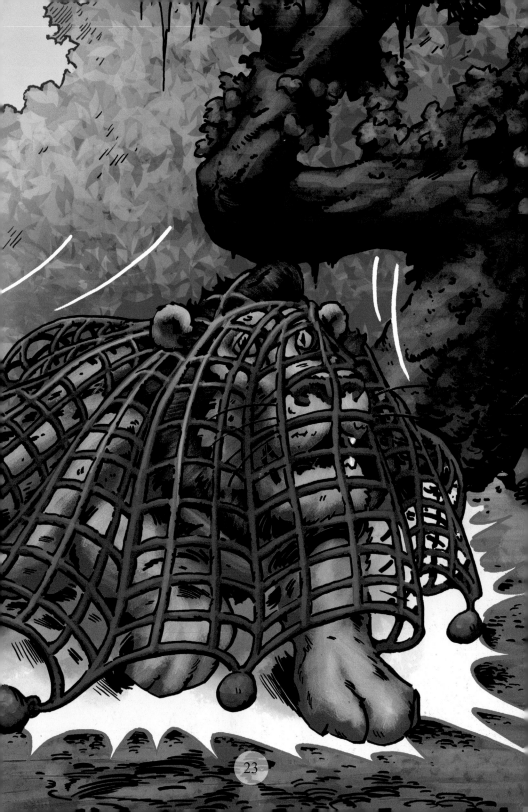

The lion roared his anger,
and the mouse heard him.

The mouse chewed through the ropes and freed the lion.

The lion was surprised the mouse had freed him.

Together, the lion and his new friend walked away.

The moral of the story is:

Little friends may prove to be great friends.